If found please return to

_____

Caregiver's Compass

Navigating Foster Care

NANCEE E. TOMLINSON

Simple Grace Publishing
P.O. Box 102
Athens, GA 30603

www.simplegracepublishing.com

ISBN: 978-1-4834-3049-2 (sc)
ISBN: 978-1-4834-3048-5 (e)

Lulu Publishing Services rev. date: 05/06/2015

Contents

Introduction

As a foster parent or caregiver for a child in the custody of CPS, you will encounter many individuals and service providers who will ask you to accomplish goals and meet expectations with which you may be unfamiliar. Managing all of these people, appointments, and expectations can be overwhelming. This journal will help you navigate the numerous people, places and appointments for which you may be responsible.

The first chapter will describe generally the type of people involved in the case, along with services provided in the most common case plans.

The second chapter will discuss the necessity of knowing the names of those who are involved in your case and their role in the progress of your case. The second chapter will include contact pages, which you can use to keep track of the individuals working on the case.

Chapter Three will discuss the general types of court dates you will encounter and will supply pages to help you keep track of these dates. The fourth chapter will focus on maintaining a list of contacts for the case and contains pages to aid you in maintaining this log. Finally, the fifth chapter will aid you in managing the case plan and your role in the case.

This book is intended to help you manage the stress you will encounter while playing this most generous role in a child's life.

Chapter 1

Basic Who and What

The role of caregivers is incredibly important. Your choice to accept responsibility for a child in need is admirable and necessary for our society to function. Stepping into this role is not always simple, though. Navigating the CPS bureaucracy and service providers along with balancing the needs, wants, and contacts of the child and the parents can be challenging.

A. The individuals generally involved in a case are listed below with a description of their role.

Judge: Attorney-appointed or elected who makes decisions in a case based on the law and the facts presented in Court. Enforces case plans, determines whether children go home.

Parents' Attorney: Either appointed to the parents or hired by the parents, this lawyer represents the parents' interests.

SAAG: The attorney who represents CPS. This person looks out for CPS's interests, which may or may not be the same as those of the caregiver.

Guardian ad litem (GAL): Attorney-appointed to look out for the child's best interests and make recommendations to the Court. These recommendations do not have to be what the child wants, only what that attorney believes are in the best interests of the child. This person might observe the child in your home.

Child's Attorney: The child will be appointed an attorney to represent the child's interests. This attorney will tell the Court what the child wants and does not take direction from you. This attorney has a different goal from the GAL.

Court Appointed Special Advocate (CASA): Community volunteer who works with children to advocate for the child's best interest. These unpaid individuals work to bond with children and give them a voice on a more daily basis to supplement the GAL's work in court. This person might observe the child in your home. CASAs do not work for CPS. They are independent.

CPS Case Manager: Person employed by CPS to make referrals for the child, to track down putative fathers, to make monthly contact with the caregiver and the child. This person makes reports to the Court about compliance with the case plan, visits, and contacts with you.

Clerk of Juvenile Court: This person works for the judge but cannot make decisions for the judge.

CPS Investigator: This person investigates allegations of abuse. This role is different from CPS Case Manager.

CPS Supervisor: The person supervising your case manager. The CPS supervisor is involved in most decisions made about each case. If you can't find your case manager, the supervisor is the person to call.

Psychologist: A doctor with a Ph.D. or Psy.D. or other approved degree who may administer tests to the child. A psychologist may also provide therapy for you and/or the child. Someone hired by CPS as an outside contractor who provides service for a fee. A psychologist may also ask to observe the child with the parent in a controlled setting as part of the parent's evaluation.

Social worker: A social worker may give tests. A social worker can provide therapy for you. Someone hired by CPS as an outside contractor who provides service for a fee.

Parent aide: A person who may supervise visits with your child, and who may provide transportation for the child-to-parent visits. This person might also provide parenting instruction.

Visitation supervisor: A person trained to observe parent visits, make notes about the visit, intervene if behaviors are not appropriate, and report to the CPS and the Court about visits.

Child Placing Agency: A private company authorized and regulated by the State. This agency may provide foster care and/or adoptive placements for children in foster care. The agency provides services to the participating placement family, including having a case manager assigned to the foster/adoptive placement in addition to the CPS case manager assigned to the case.

Care Coordinator: The State licenses private agencies to provide many of the mental health and family services mentioned in this book. Each private agency will assign a person to locate appropriate services and make contact with clients maintain consistent treatment.

B. Description & Types of Appointments

Case Plan: The list of steps and goals proposed by CPS to the Court. A parent or a child, through counsel, can request modifications to the proposed case plan when needed. The list will include all of the steps for a parent to obtain custody of their child. The case plan will also include medical treatment for the child as well as psychological testing and therapy where appropriate. Also, the judge's instructions about the limits on visitation with parents, at least initially, will be written out.

CCFA: Comprehensive Child and Family Assessment. This report will be based on interviews with family, friends, teachers (where appropriate), alternate caregivers, evaluation of the parents' home, discussion of the family's and child's history; it will generally make recommendations from a social work perspective on how best to reunite the family.

Psychological Evaluation: This report is a compilation of psychological testing conducted at the direction of a psychologist. These tests will include written scales (evaluation), verbal testing, and observation. The psychological evaluation requires four steps. First, an appointment must be scheduled with the psychologist. Second, the patient must complete all testing. Third, you must schedule and attend another appointment during which you review the evaluation with the psychologist. You should attend an appointment during which the patient and any guardian will review the evaluation with the psychologist to learn the results of the testing. The psychologist will make recommendations for further treatment. These recommendations will become part of the case plan. If a parent or child or caregiver has questions about these recommendations, this fourth appointment is the time to ask the questions.

CSI: Community Support for Individuals. This service is for behavioral support and is funded by Medicaid. The provider is usually an individual with a Masters Degree in Social Work. Behavioral support will be in the vein of therapy and behavior modification through appropriate methods. The service provider may meet with the child or adolescent in the home or at school. CSI is a very low level of intervention.

IFI: Intensive Family Intervention, also known as Iffy. A service provided by Medicaid to children and adolescents. IFI provides in-home/in-school therapy, behavioral coaching, and parent support to children at risk for being hospitalized for mental health or behavior issues. IFI serves children at risk for hospitalization, who have recently been discharged from an out-of-community placement (hospital or group home), or for whom the intensive therapy, coaching, and parent support are recommended to avoid an out-of-community placement. Initially, IFI will continue for 12 weeks. Service providers may request additional time if the services are resulting in signs of improvement. The service is provided by specialists and led by a licensed clinician. IFI is the highest level of community-based intervention available through Medicaid.

PRTF: Psychiatric Residential Treatment Facility. To have a child or adult committed to a mental health facility, a doctor must make an application to APS or their insurance provider. APS Healthcare is a privacy agency charged with approving treatment plans for traditional Medicaid providers and with auditing agencies for financial and clinical practice.

APS evaluates the child/adult based on admission criteria. Approval by APS does not mean automatic placement in a facility. A child must have a proven record of a failure of community-based services to meet the child's needs. The exception is when a person is an imminent threat to themselves or others.

Medical Evaluations: Each child who enters CPS custody will have a medical evaluation, which would also include dental evaluation.

Family Team Meeting: A meeting to discuss how to reunite the family. The parents, the child (depending on age), the CPS workers, CASA, and Guardian ad litem will be included. Ideas for a case plan may also come from this meeting.

<u>Staffing:</u> A meeting where CPS talks about the progress of the case and what steps should be taken to accomplish reunification. CPS might include the SAAG, the Guardian ad litem, and the CASA. In some instances, the staffing might result in decisions about non-reunification and adoption options as well.

Chapter 2

Names and Contact Information

As described in Chapter 1, you will encounter a number of people. The law now requires the presence of the child at court, which may require that you transport the child. In those instances you are more likely to meet these people.

You will notice below that there are multiple entries for Case Manager. Over time, the case manager may change several times. The reasons for this may vary, but the reality of the situation is that the case manager will change.

Court Personnel

Child's Name _____

Name of Child's Attorney_____

Attorney Phone Number _____

Guardian ad Litem_____

    Guardian ad Litem's Phone Number _____

CASA Name _____

    CASA Phone Number _____

Judge's Name _____

    Court's Phone Number _____

Case Manager _____

    Case Manager's Phone Number _____

Case Manager _____

    Case Manager's Phone Number _____

Case Manager _____

    Case Manager's Phone Number _____

Case Manager _____

    Case Manager's Phone Number _____

Case Manager _____

    Case Manager's Phone Number _____

Case Manager _____

    Case Manager's Phone Number _____

Case Manager **Supervisor's** Name _____

Case Manager's Supervisor's Phone Number _____

Child Placing Agency

Name of Child Placing Agency _____

Phone Number _____

Agency Case Manager's Name _____

Agency Case Manager's Number: _____

Other Agency Information _____

_____

_____

Treatment Providers

CCFA Evaluator _____

CCFA Evaluator's Phone Number _____

Therapist Name _____

Therapist's Phone Number _____

Parent Aide Name _____

Parent Aide's Phone Number _____

Visitation Supervisor _____

    Visitation Supervisor's Phone Number _____

Child's Medical Doctor _____

    Child's Medical Doctor's Phone Number _____

Child's Psychologist _____

    Child's Psychologist's Phone Number _____

Child's Therapist Name _____

    Child's Therapist's Phone Number _____

Care Coordinating Agency _____

Care Coordinator _____

    Care Coordinator's Phone Number: _____

Name of Child's School _____

    Principal's Name _____

    School Phone Number _____

    Teacher's Name _____

    Teacher's Email _____

    Teacher's Contact Phone Number _____

Chapter 3

Court Appearances

Navigating court appearances can be a challenge. The names of hearings do not always provide an accurate idea of what will be happening in court.

Always prepare for court appearances to take longer than planned. Attorneys will be negotiating a possible resolution. Hearings may be continued, that is, postponed to a future date, without much notice. The various attorneys may ask to speak with you or with the child. If the child has an attorney, consult that attorney about any meetings.

A. Court Order and Appearance Names

Safety Plan: In some cases CPS decides to work with parents to resolve issues before removing a child legally from a parent's care. The Safety Plan is an agreement between parents and CPS. Sometimes as a part of the Safety Plan, a child will be placed with a family member or friend as a caregiver resource. The caregiver resource must follow the Safety Plan, too.

Removal Order: When CPS presents the Court with facts that support removing a child from a home. The order may initially be issued over the phone, but a written order including the Court's finding of facts must be filed with the Court.

Shelter Care: This hearing may be referred to as a Preliminary Hearing or a 72-hour hearing. CPS must notify the parents of the time and place of this hearing. The hearing should be conducted within 72 hours of the child's being taken into CPS custody, though a deadline falling on a weekend or holiday will be considered to fall on the next business day. Any person interested in the child's welfare would be among those who may be present and may be heard on the issues in this hearing.

The Court must determine if there is probable cause to keep the child in CPS custody based on evidence relating to abuse or neglect of the child. If there is such a finding, the child will remain in care until the Dependency Hearing. Or, the Court could find that there is no probable cause and release the child back to the parents.

Dependency Hearing: CPS and their attorney must prove at this hearing by clear and convincing evidence that the child needs to be in care of CPS while the parents work to remedy the problems in the home due to abuse or neglect of the child.

Disposition Hearing: At this hearing, CPS will present a proposed case plan and the Court will order the parents and CPS to accomplish the goals of the case plan. Understand that some of the goals will be matters related to the child's health, education, and welfare. Caregivers should pay close attention to these goals. Be sure to ask questions if subjects are unclear.

Reviews: These periodic hearings provide the Judge an opportunity to cajole parents, scold CPS for falling short, praise parents for progress, tweak case plans when requested, and generally keep track of the case plan progress. Each judge has his or her own schedule for holding these review hearings; they occur sometimes every three months, sometimes every six months.

Citizens' Review Panel: In some jurisdictions, a group of concerned citizens is appointed by the Court to review case plans instead of the Judge. The panel may want to hear from the caregiver and the child when appropriate. The parents will be invited and likely present at the panel meeting. The decision of the panel may be appealed to the juvenile court. The Judge could change the outcome if the Court disagrees with the Panel's recommendations.

Termination of Parental Rights: When a parent fails to substantially complete a case plan, CPS files a Petition to Terminate Parental Rights. Termination is the final severing of parental rights and legal ties between parent and child. The Court will be cautious in proceeding to this point in the case. Understand that this process takes time. Attorneys will fight harder to avoid termination for parents. The termination may be set and continued a couple of times before the hearing is finally completed. Caregivers testify in these hearings about the current circumstances of the child. Be prepared to testify as to how the child is doing in school, who provides therapy, what if any medical conditions and medications the child may have.

Court dates will happen fast and furiously during the early stages of the case. After a finding of dependency, dates will be further apart. Being present for court, as a caregiver, is a right but not a requirement. If you have concerns about the child, you should be there to voice those concerns.

Post Termination Review: These hearings will continue to occur until the child is adopted. As long as the child remains in the legal custody of CPS, the Court will maintain a schedule of reviews to ensure the child's welfare. The parents will not be part of these proceedings, as their rights have been terminated.

B. Court Dates

Below you will find spaces for the resetting of some early court dates because many times a case has to be rescheduled for a myriad of reasons. If the continuance causes a concern for the child, please notify the CASA and/or Guardian ad Litem.

Note that some courts use Citizen Review Panels instead of frequent reviews in front of the Judge. Feel free to modify the interim reviews (3, 9, 15, 21) to reflect Citizen Review Panel.

Shelter Care Hearing: _____

Reset of Shelter Care Hearing: _____

Dependency Hearing: _____

Reset of Dependency Hearing: _____

Disposition Hearing: _____

Reset of Disposition Hearing: _____

3 month Review: _____

6 month Review: _____

9 month Review: _____

12 month Review: _____

15 month Review: _____

18 month Review: _____

21 month Review: _____

24 month Review: _____

Termination Hearing: _____

Reset of Termination Hearing: _____

Post Termination Review: _____

Chapter 4

Maintaining a Record

One of your jobs as a caregiver is maintaining appointments for the child. You must keep track of doctors, teachers, CPS employees, lawyers, and CASAs. Remembering who said what to you could become overwhelming.

In the following pages, you can maintain a journal of whom you contacted or attempted to contact. This journal will aid you with reporting to the Court or to CPS about who saw this child and what you were told by the provider about this child.

You may encounter repeated efforts to call individuals without return calls or lack of follow-up by people with whom you've spoken, and you should keep a written record of these. This record, if used by you as habit and routine, will be useful and reliable in your efforts to protect this child.

You will find that these pages provide a good reminder in times that might be stressful. Stress makes the memory work slower. These notes will refresh your memory to enhance your reporting to the bureaucracy. If you run out of contact entries in this book, please purchase a notebook in which to continue your efforts.

CONTACT LOG

Date: _____ Time: _____

Contact: _____

Phone Number: _____

Notes:_____

_____

_____

_____

Date: _____ Time: _____

Contact: _____

Phone Number: _____

Notes:_____

_____

_____

_____

Date: _____ Time: _____

Contact: _____

Phone Number: _____

Notes:_____

_____

_____

Date: _____ Time: _____

Contact: _____

Phone Number: _____

Notes:_____

_____

_____

_____

Date: _____ Time: _____

Contact: _____

Phone Number: _____

Notes:_____

_____

_____

_____

Date: _____ Time: _____

Contact: _____

Phone Number: _____

Notes:_____

_____

_____

_____

Nancee E. Tomlinson

Date: _____ Time: _____

Contact: _____

Phone Number: _____

Notes:_____

_____

_____

_____

Date: _____ Time: _____

Contact: _____

Phone Number: _____

Notes:_____

_____

_____

_____

Date: _____ Time: _____

Contact: _____

Phone Number: _____

Notes:_____

_____

_____

_____

Date: _____ Time: _____

Contact: _____

Phone Number: _____

Notes:_____

_____

_____

_____

Date: _____ Time: _____

Contact: _____

Phone Number: _____

Notes:_____

_____

_____

_____

Date: _____ Time: _____

Contact: _____

Phone Number: _____

Notes:_____

_____

_____

_____

Date: _____ Time: _____

Contact: _____

Phone Number: _____

Notes:_____

_____

_____

_____

Date: _____ Time: _____

Contact: _____

Phone Number: _____

Notes:_____

_____

_____

_____

Date: _____ Time: _____

Contact: _____

Phone Number: _____

Notes:_____

_____

_____

_____

Date: _____ Time: _____

Contact: _____

Phone Number: _____

Notes:_____

_____

_____

_____

Date: _____ Time: _____

Contact: _____

Phone Number: _____

Notes:_____

_____

_____

_____

Date: _____ Time: _____

Contact: _____

Phone Number: _____

Notes:_____

_____

_____

_____

Date: _____ Time: _____

Contact: _____

Phone Number: _____

Notes:_____

_____

_____

_____

Date: _____ Time: _____

Contact: _____

Phone Number: _____

Notes:_____

_____

_____

_____

Date: _____ Time: _____

Contact: _____

Phone Number: _____

Notes:_____

_____

_____

_____

Date: _____ Time: _____

Contact: _____

Phone Number: _____

Notes:_____

_____

_____

_____

Date: _____ Time: _____

Contact: _____

Phone Number: _____

Notes:_____

_____

_____

_____

Date: _____ Time: _____

Contact: _____

Phone Number: _____

Notes:_____

_____

_____

_____

Date: _____ Time: _____

Contact: _____

Phone Number: _____

Notes:_____

_____

_____

_____

Date: _____ Time: _____

Contact: _____

Phone Number: _____

Notes:_____

_____

_____

_____

Date: _____ Time: _____

Contact: _____

Phone Number: _____

Notes:_____

_____

_____

_____

Date: _____ Time: _____

Contact: _____

Phone Number: _____

Notes:_____

_____

_____

_____

Date: _____ Time: _____

Contact: _____

Phone Number: _____

Notes:_____

_____

_____

_____

Date: _____ Time: _____

Contact: _____

Phone Number: _____

Notes:_____

_____

_____

_____

Date: _____ Time: _____

Contact: _____

Phone Number: _____

Notes:_____

_____

_____

_____

Date: _____ Time: _____

Contact: _____

Phone Number: _____

Notes:_____

_____

_____

_____

Date: _____ Time: _____

Contact: _____

Phone Number: _____

Notes:_____

_____

_____

_____

Date: _____ Time: _____

Contact: _____

Phone Number: _____

Notes:_____

_____

_____

_____

Date: _____ Time: _____

Contact: _____

Phone Number: _____

Notes:_____

_____

_____

_____

Date: _____ Time: _____

Contact: _____

Phone Number: _____

Notes:_____

_____

_____

_____

Date: _____ Time: _____

Contact: _____

Phone Number: _____

Notes:_____

_____

_____

_____

Date: _____ Time: _____

Contact: _____

Phone Number: _____

Notes:_____

_____

_____

_____

Date: _____ Time: _____

Contact: _____

Phone Number: _____

Notes:_____

_____

_____

_____

Date: _____ Time: _____

Contact: _____

Phone Number: _____

Notes:_____

_____

_____

_____

Date: _____ Time: _____

Contact: _____

Phone Number: _____

Notes:_____

_____

_____

_____

Date: _____ Time: _____

Contact: _____

Phone Number: _____

Notes:_____

_____

_____

_____

Date: _____ Time: _____

Contact: _____

Phone Number: _____

Notes:_____

_____

_____

_____

Date: _____ Time: _____

Contact: _____

Phone Number: _____

Notes:_____

_____

_____

_____

Date: _____ Time: _____

Contact: _____

Phone Number: _____

Notes:_____

_____

_____

_____

Date: _____ Time: _____

Contact: _____

Phone Number: _____

Notes:_____

_____

_____

_____

Date: _____ Time: _____

Contact: _____

Phone Number: _____

Notes:_____

_____

_____

_____

Date: _____ Time: _____

Contact: _____

Phone Number: _____

Notes:_____

_____

_____

_____

Date: _____ Time: _____

Contact: _____

Phone Number: _____

Notes:_____

_____

_____

_____

Date: _____ Time: _____

Contact: _____

Phone Number: _____

Notes:_____

_____

_____

_____

Date: _____ Time: _____

Contact: _____

Phone Number: _____

Notes:_____

_____

_____

_____

Date: _____ Time: _____

Contact: _____

Phone Number: _____

Notes:_____

_____

_____

_____

Date: _____ Time: _____

Contact: _____

Phone Number: _____

Notes:_____

_____

_____

_____

Date: _____ Time: _____

Contact: _____

Phone Number: _____

Notes:_____

_____

_____

_____

Date: _____ Time: _____

Contact: _____

Phone Number: _____

Notes:_____

_____

_____

_____

Date: _____ Time: _____

Contact: _____

Phone Number: _____

Notes:_____

_____

_____

_____

Date: _____ Time: _____

Contact: _____

Phone Number: _____

Notes:_____

_____

_____

_____

Chapter 5

Tracking Obligations

You should receive a copy of the Case Plan for the child. If you do not, request a copy from CPS. If they are unwilling, the Child's attorney or Guardian ad litem should provide a copy for the child.

Knowing the requirements of the Case Plan helps you keep track of what you will need to facilitate for the child. Also, this plan helps you respond to concerns that the child might have.

Also, for goals that are unfamiliar to you, find out how many steps may be involved. Making a doctor's appointment is routine. Setting up a psychological evaluation may require more steps. Remember to notify CPS of appointments as well.

Case Plan Goal 1: _____

Goal for whom: (circle one) Parent Child CPS

Action required for Goal: _____

_____

_____ Goal Accomplished (check off when completed)

Case Plan Goal 2: _____

Goal for whom: (circle one) Parent Child CPS

Action required for Goal: _____

_____

_____ Goal Accomplished (check off when completed)

Case Plan Goal 3: _____

Goal for whom: (circle one) Parent Child CPS

Action required for Goal: _____

_____

_____ Goal Accomplished (check off when completed)

Case Plan Goal 4: _____

Goal for whom: (circle one) Parent Child CPS

Action required for Goal: _____

_____

_____ Goal Accomplished (check off when completed)

Case Plan Goal 5: _____

Goal for whom: (circle one) Parent Child CPS

Action required for Goal: _____

_____

_____ Goal Accomplished (check off when completed)

Case Plan Goal 6: _____

Goal for whom: (circle one) Parent Child CPS

Action required for Goal: _____

_____

_____ Goal Accomplished (check off when completed)

Case Plan Goal 7: _____

Goal for whom: (circle one) Parent Child CPS

Action required for Goal: _____

_____

_____ Goal Accomplished (check off when completed)

Case Plan Goal 8: _____

Goal for whom: (circle one) Parent Child CPS

Action required for Goal: _____

_____

_____ Goal Accomplished (check off when completed)

Case Plan Goal 9: _____

Goal for whom: (circle one) Parent Child CPS

Action required for Goal: _____

_____

_____ Goal Accomplished (check off when completed)

Case Plan Goal 10: _____

Goal for whom: (circle one) Parent Child CPS

Action required for Goal: _____

_____

_____ Goal Accomplished (check off when completed)

Chapter 6

Parting Thoughts

Caregivers often do not understand their role in the process. CPS has custody or has executed a safety plan to protect a child. When CPS has custody, the case plan, the Judge, and CPS direct what you can and cannot do for the child. You may provide for the child's personal needs beyond whatever funding may be granted through CPS. Treat the child as one of your own. This child needs love, support, stability, and caring through this separation from parents.

If a safety plan rather than a dependency case plan is in place, understand that you have agreed to follow the safety plan to protect this child. Legally, the parent may still have custody, but your obligation is to the child and to the agreement with CPS. If you want a long-term relationship with this child, bending to the parent's will when it contradicts the CPS safety plan will forever damage your relationship with CPS. That damage could prevent a long-term placement with you if the parent fails to complete their aspects of the safety plan.

As a caregiver, your obligation is to protect this child. If you have concerns for the child, contact the child's attorney, the GAL, or the CASA. Each of these people speaks for the child. CPS may not be as responsive as you think they should be. These advocates are specially placed just for the child.

CPS case managers flow in and out of CPS offices. That is a fact of life in this industry. Keeping up with the case manager and keeping a case manager up to date is important. Using this guide to record the history of the case will help you keep everything straight. Knowing the history for the child is critical to meeting the child's needs.

Glossary

This glossary serves as a quick reference guide for the terms used in the book. The definitions are exactly the same and located at the back of the book for ease of location.

Care Coordinator: The State licenses private agencies to provide many of the mental health and family services mentioned in this book. Each private agency will assign a person to locate appropriate services and make contact with clients maintain consistent treatment.

CASA-Court Appointed Special Advocate: Community volunteers who work with children to advocate for the child's best interest. These unpaid individuals work to bond with children and give them a voice on a more daily basis to supplement the GAL's work in court. This person might observe the child in your home. CASAs do not work for CPS. They are independent.

Case Plan: The list of steps and goals proposed by CPS to the Court. A parent or a child, through counsel, can request modifications to the proposed case plan when needed. The list will include all of the steps for a parent to obtain custody of their child. The case plan will also include medical treatment for the child as well as psychological testing and therapy where appropriate. Also, the judge's instructions about the limits on visitation with parents, at least initially, will be written out.

Child Placing Agency: A private company authorized and regulated by the State. This agency may provide foster care and/or adoptive placements for children in foster care. The agency provides services to the participating placement family, including having a case manager assigned to the foster/adoptive placement in addition to the CPS case manager assigned to the case.

Child's Attorney: The child will be appointed an attorney to represent the child's interests. This attorney will tell the Court what the child wants and does not take direction from you. This attorney has a different goal from the GAL.

Citizens' Review Panel: In some jurisdictions, a group of concerned citizens is appointed by the Court to review case plans instead of the Judge. The panel may want to hear from the caregiver and the child when appropriate. The parents will be invited and likely present at the panel meeting. The decision of the panel may be appealed to the juvenile court. The Judge could change the outcome if the Court disagrees with the Panel's recommendations.

Clerk of Juvenile Court: This person works for the judge but cannot make decisions for the judge.

CPS Case Manager: Person employed by CPS to make referrals for the child, to track down putative fathers, to make monthly contact with the caregiver and the child. This person makes reports to the Court about compliance with the case plan, visits, and contacts with you.

CPS Investigator: This person investigates allegations of abuse. This role is different from CPS Case Manager.

CPS Supervisor: The person supervising your case manager. The CPS supervisor is involved in most decisions made about each case. If you can't find your case manager, the supervisor is the person to call.

CSI: Community Support for Individuals. This service is for behavioral support and is funded by Medicaid. The provider is usually an individual with a Masters Degree in Social Work. Behavioral support will be in the vein of therapy and behavior modification through appropriate methods. The service provider may meet with the child or adolescent in the home or at school. CSI is a very low level of intervention.

CCFA: Comprehensive Child and Family Assessment. This report will be based on interviews with family, friends, teachers (where appropriate), alternate caregivers, evaluating the parents' home, discussing the family's and child's history, and generally making recommendations from a social work perspective on how best to reunite the family.

Dependency Hearing: CPS and their attorney must prove at this hearing by clear and convincing evidence that the child needs to be in care of CPS while the parents work to remedy the problems of abuse or neglect of the child in the home.

Disposition Hearing: At this hearing, CPS will present a proposed case plan and the Court will order the parents and CPS to accomplish the goals of the case plan. Understand that some of the goals will be matters related to the child's health, education, and welfare. Caregivers should pay close attention to these goals. Be sure to ask questions if subjects are unclear.

Family Team Meeting: A meeting to discuss how to reunite the family. The parents, the child (depending on age), the CPS workers, CASA and Guardian ad litem will be included. Ideas for a case plan may also come from this meeting.

Guardian ad litem (GAL): Attorney-appointed to look out for the child's best interests and make recommendations to the Court. These recommendations do not have to be what the child wants, only what that attorney believes are in the best interests of the child. This person might observe the child in your home.

IFI: Intensive Family Intervention, also known as Iffy. A service provided by Medicaid to children and adolescents. IFI provides in home/in school therapy, behavioral coaching, and parent support to children at risk for being hospitalized for mental health or behavior issues. IFI serves children at risk for hospitalization, who have recently been discharged from an out-of-community placement (hospital or group home), or for whom the intensive therapy, coaching and parent support are recommended to avoid an out-of-community placement. Initially, IFI will continue for 12 weeks. Service providers may request additional time if the services are showing signs of improvement. The service is provided by specialists and led by a licensed clinician. IFI is the highest level of community-based intervention available through Medicaid.

Judge: Attorney-appointed or -elected who makes decisions in a case based on the law and the facts presented in Court. Enforces case plans, determines whether children go home.

Medical Evaluations: Each child who enters CPS custody will have a medical evaluation, which would also include dental evaluation.

Parent aide: A person who may supervise visits with your child, and who may provide transportation for the child-to-parent visits. This person might also provide parenting instruction.

Parents' Attorney: Either appointed to the parents or hired by the parents, this lawyer represents the parents' interests.

Post Termination Review: These hearings will continue to occur until the child is adopted. As long as the child remains in the legal custody of CPS, the Court will maintain a schedule of reviews to insure the child's welfare. The parents will not be part of these proceedings, as their rights have been terminated.

PRTF: Psychiatric Residential Treatment Facility. To have a child or adult committed to a mental health facility, a doctor must make an application to APS or their insurance provider. APS Healthcare is a privacy agency charged with approving treatment plans for traditional Medicaid providers and with auditing agencies for financial and clinical practice.

APS evaluates the child/adult based on admission criteria. Approval by APS does not mean automatic placement in a facility. There must be a proven record of a failure of community-based services to meet the child's needs. The exception is when a person is an imminent threat to themselves or others.

Psychological Evaluation: This report is a compilation of psychological testing conducted at the direction of a psychologist. These tests will include written scales (evaluation), verbal testing and observation. The psychological evaluation requires four steps. First, an appointment must be scheduled with the psychologist. Second, the patient must complete all testing. Third, you must schedule and attend another appointment during which you review the evaluation with the psychologist. You should attend an appointment during which the patient and any guardian will review the evaluation with the psychologist to learn the results of the testing. The psychologist will make recommendations for further treatment. These recommendations will become part of the case plan. If a parent or child or caregiver has questions about these recommendations, this fourth appointment is the time to ask the questions.

Psychologist: A doctor with a Ph.D. or Psy.D. or other approved degree who may administer tests to the child. A psychologist may also provide therapy for you and/or the child. Someone hired by CPS as an outside contractor who provides service for a fee. A psychologist may also ask to observe the child with the parent in a controlled setting as part of the parent's evaluation.

Removal Order: When CPS presents the Court with facts that support removing a child from a home. The order may initially be issued over the phone, but a written order including the Court's finding of facts must be filed with the Court.

Reviews: These periodic hearings provide the Judge an opportunity to cajole parents, scold CPS for falling short, praise parents for progress, tweak case plans when requested, and generally keep track of the case plan progress. Each judge has his or her own schedule for holding these review hearings; they occur sometimes every three months, sometimes every six months.

SAAG-Special Assistant Attorney General: The attorney who represents CPS. This person looks out for CPS's interests, which may or may not be the same as those of the caregiver.

Safety Plan: In some cases CPS decides to work with parents to resolve issues before removing a child legally from a parent's care. The Safety Plan is an agreement between parents and CPS. Sometimes as a part of the Safety Plan, a child will be placed with a family member or friend as a caregiver resource. The caregiver resource must follow the Safety Plan, too.

Shelter Care: This hearing may be referred to as a Preliminary Hearing or a 72-hour hearing. CPS must notify the parents of the time and place of this hearing. The hearing should be conducted within 72 hours of the child's being taken into CPS custody, though a deadline falling on a weekend or holiday will be considered to fall on the next business day. Any person interested in the child's welfare would be among those who may be present and may be heard on the issues in this hearing.

The Court must determine if there is probable cause to keep the child in CPS custody based on evidence relating to abuse or neglect of the child. If there is such a ruling, the child will remain in care until the Dependency Hearing. Or, the Court could find that there is no probable cause and release the child back to the parents.

Social worker: A social worker may give tests. A social worker can provide therapy for you. Someone hired by CPS as an outside contractor who provides service for a fee.

Staffing: A meeting where CPS talks about the progress of the case and what steps should be taken to accomplish reunification. CPS might include the SAAG, the Guardian ad litem, and the CASA. In some instances, the staffing might result in decisions about non-reunification and adoption options as well.

Termination of Parental Rights: When a parent fails to substantially complete a case plan, CPS files a Petition to Terminate Parental Rights. Termination is the final severing of parental rights and legal ties between parent and child. The Court will be cautious in proceeding to this point in the case. Understand that this process takes time. Attorneys will fight harder to avoid termination for parents. The termination may be set and continued a couple of times before the hearing is finally completed. Caregivers testify in these hearings about the current circumstances of the child. Be prepared to testify how the child is doing in school, who provides therapy, what if any medical conditions and medications the child may have.

Visitation supervisor: A person trained to observe parent visits, make notes about the visit, intervene if behaviors are not appropriate, and report to the CPS and the Court about visits.

www.ingramcontent.com/pod-product-compliance
Lightning Source LLC
Chambersburg PA
CBHW021923170526
45157CB00005B/2158

9781483430492